HISTORY'S MOST INFLUENTIAL

WRITERS

FROM THE Early 1900s TO THE Mid-1900s

Rabindranath Tagore to George Orwell

EDITED BY J.E. LUEBERING

Britannica® Educational Publishing

IN ASSOCIATION WITH

ROSEN

EDUCATIONAL SERVICES

Published in 2025 by Britannica Educational Publishing
(a trademark of Encyclopædia Britannica, Inc.)
in association with Rosen Educational Services, LLC
2544 Clinton Street, Buffalo, NY 14224.

Distributed exclusively by Rosen Educational Services.
For a listing of additional Britannica Educational Publishing titles, call toll free (800) 237-9932.

First Edition

Britannica Educational Publishing
Michael I. Levy: Executive Editor
Marilyn L. Barton: Senior Coordinator, Production Control
Steven Bosco: Director, Editorial Technologies
Lisa S. Braucher: Senior Producer and Data Editor
Yvette Charboneau: Senior Copy Editor
Kathy Nakamura: Manager, Media Acquisition
J. E. Luebering: Manager and Senior Editor, Literature

Editor: Greg Roza
Book design: Michael Flynn

Photo credits: Cover https://commons.wikimedia.org/wiki/File:Virginia_Woolf_1927.jpg; p. 7 https://commons.wikimedia.org/wiki/File:Rabindranath_Tagore_in_1909.jpg; p. 27 https://commons.wikimedia.org/wiki/File:George_Charles_Beresford_-_Virginia_Woolf_in_1902_-_Restoration.jpg; p. 40 Pandora Pictures/Shutterstock.com; p. 56 https://commons.wikimedia.org/wiki/File:Ernest_Hemingway_Writing_at_Campsite_in_Kenya_-_NARA_-_192655.jpg.

Cataloging-in-Publication Data

Names: Luebering, J.E.
Title: From the early 1900s to the mid-1900s: Rabindranath Tagore to George Orwell / edited by J.E. Luebering.
Description: New York : Britannica Educational Publishing, in Association with Rosen Educational Services, 2025. | Series: History's most influential writers | Includes glossary and index.
Identifiers: ISBN 9781641901147 (library bound) | ISBN 9781641901130 (pbk) | ISBN 9781641901154 (ebook)
Subjects: LCSH: Authors--20th century--Biography. | Authorship--History--20th century.
Classification: LCC PN451.F766 2025 | DDC 809'.04 B --dc23

Manufactured in the United States of America

CPSIA Compliance Information: Batch #CSBRIT25. For further information contact Rosen Publishing at 1-800-237-9932.

CONTENTS

INTRODUCTION

"So long as you write what you wish to write, that is all that matters; and whether it matters for the ages or only for hours, nobody can say."
—Virginia Woolf (1882–1941)

Open a book—any book. In it you'll find words, of course, but look closely and you'll also find art, crafted, in detail, by a writer proud enough to sign his or her name to the work. In a book, or in any piece of writing, words are joined together at the whim of the author. Sentences are created, paragraphs and stanzas formatted, chapters built, and stories told. In a book or a poem, a play or a short story, everything is there, on the page, for a reason: To show, to tell, to convey a message. Most works of writing, quite simply, are meant for reading. The great ones, however, by the most talented and ingenious authors, are for study. In such works, it's the art one finds within that sets them apart from the rest.

Writers are influenced by the places in which they live and the cultures in which they are steeped. The writers in this volume lived during the early 1900s and mid-1900s. Several individuals included in this volume, such as Virginia Woolf and Ernest Hemingway, are paradigms of English literature. Others wrote in their native tongues in Italy, France, Germany, China, and Russia.

As the title of this book indicates, all those featured in this collection are influential writers. Through their work, they reached out to the masses, touched the hearts and souls of millions, and left their mark on the world. But how exactly is influence defined in this case? Perhaps it's the ability of one person, through his or her writing, to change the way the world thinks. For example, Lu Xun, the founder of modern Chinese literature, had a huge influence on Communism in that country.

Perhaps a writer's influence is determined by timeless prominence, the ability to remain relevant hundreds of years after initial publication. All of the authors in this book fit that bill. This ability to sway audiences so deeply, and in so many ways, several centuries after the fact is arguably the very definition of influential.

With carefully crafted prose or a verse, a writer can influence individual allegiances, support or defame a political regime, or effect change by shedding light on an untenable situation. When all is said and done, perhaps what makes a writer influential is simply the ability to entertain, to keep readers up at night, turning page after page, just so they can learn what happens next.

The truth is, influence can mean so many things and can be measured in so many ways. Those who read the works of any of the writers profiled in this book may very well discover an experience they've perhaps never had before. They might have their imagination sparked and be transported, however briefly, from the travails of the life they're living. An author's writing might, with its insight, highlight an injustice, leading readers to speak out themselves and demand an equitable resolution. Whatever the case, one can't read a work by authors such as those detailed here without being influenced in some way. That's the power of great writing. And that's the real reason we read.

RABINDRANATH TAGORE

(b. May 7, 1861, Calcutta, India—d. Aug. 7, 1941, Calcutta)

Rabindranath Tagore, a Bengali poet, short-story writer, song composer, playwright, essayist, and painter, was awarded the Nobel Prize for Literature in 1913. Tagore introduced new prose and verse forms and the use of colloquial language into Bengali literature, thereby freeing it from traditional models based on classical Sanskrit. He was highly influential in introducing the best of Indian culture to the West and vice versa, and he is generally regarded as the outstanding creative artist of modern India.

The son of the religious reformer Debendranath Tagore, he early began to write verses. After incomplete studies in England in the late 1870s, he returned to India. There he published several books of poetry in the 1880s and completed *Mānasī* (1890), a collection that marks the maturing of his genius. It contains some of his best-known poems, including many in verse forms new to Bengali, as well as some social and political satire that was critical of his fellow Bengalis.

In 1891 Tagore went to East Bengal (now in Bangladesh) to manage his family's estates at Shilaidah and Shazadpur for 10 years. There he often stayed in a houseboat on the Padma River (i.e., the Ganges River), in close contact with village folk, and his sympathy for their poverty and backwardness became the keynote of much of his later writing. Most of his finest short stories, which examine "humble lives and their small miseries," date from the 1890s and have a poignancy, laced with gentle irony, that is unique to him, though admirably captured by the director Satyajit Ray in later film adaptations. Tagore came to love the Bengali countryside, most of all the Padma River, an

Bengali poet and short-story writer Rabindranath Tagore bridged the gap between East and West with groundbreaking, influential prose and verse.

often-repeated image in his verse. During these years he published several poetry collections, notably *Sonār Tarī* (1894; *The Golden Boat*), and plays, notably *Chitrāngadā* (1892; *Chitra*). Tagore's poems are virtually untranslatable, as are his more than 2,000 songs, which remain extremely popular among all classes of Bengali society.

In 1901 Tagore founded an experimental school in rural West Bengal at *Śantiniketan* ("Abode of Peace"), where he sought to blend the best in the Indian and Western traditions. He settled permanently at the school, which became Viśva-Bhārati University in 1921. Years of sadness arising from the deaths of his wife and two children between 1902 and 1907 are reflected in his later poetry, which was introduced to the West in *Gitanjali, Song Offerings* (1912). This book, containing Tagore's English prose translations of religious poems from several of his Bengali verse collections, including *Gītāñjali* (1910), was hailed by W. B. Yeats and André Gide and won him the Nobel Prize in 1913. Tagore was awarded a knighthood in 1915, but he repudiated it in 1919 as a protest against the Amritsar Massacre.

From 1912 Tagore spent long periods out of India, lecturing and reading from his work in Europe, the Americas, and East Asia and becoming an eloquent spokesperson for the cause of Indian independence. Tagore's novels, though less outstanding than his poems and short stories, are also worthy of attention; the best known are *Gorā* (1910) and *Ghare-Bāire* (1916; *The Home and the World*). In the late 1920s, at nearly 70 years of age, Tagore took up painting and produced works that won him a place among India's foremost contemporary artists.

WILLIAM BUTLER YEATS

(b. June 13, 1865, Sandymount, Dublin, Ire.—d. Jan. 28, 1939, Roquebrune-Cap-Martin, France)

The Irish poet, dramatist, and prose writer William Butler Yeats was one of the greatest English-language poets of the 20th century. He received the Nobel Prize for Literature in 1923.

In 1867, when Yeats was only two, his family moved to London, but he spent much of his boyhood and school holidays in Sligo, in western Ireland, with his grandparents. This country—its scenery, folklore, and supernatural legend—would color Yeats's work and form the setting of many of his poems. In 1880 his family moved back to Dublin, where he attended the high school. In 1883 he attended the Metropolitan School of Art in Dublin, where the most important part of his education was in meeting other poets and artists.

Meanwhile, Yeats was beginning to write. His first publication, two brief lyrics, appeared in the *Dublin University Review* in 1885. When the family moved back to London in 1887, Yeats took up the life of a professional writer. He joined the Theosophical Society, whose mysticism appealed to him because it was a form of imaginative life far removed from the workaday world. His early poems, collected in *The Wanderings of Oisin, and Other Poems* (1889), are the work of an aesthete, often beautiful but always rarefied, a soul's cry for release from circumstance.

Yeats quickly became involved in the literary life of London. He became friends with William Morris and W. E. Henley, and he was a cofounder of the Rhymers' Club, whose members included his friends Lionel Johnson and Arthur Symons. In 1889 Yeats met Maud Gonne, an Irish beauty, ardent and brilliant. He fell in love with her, but she was not in love with him. Her passion was lavished upon Ireland; she was an Irish patriot, a rebel, and a rhetorician, commanding in voice and in person. When Yeats joined in the Irish nationalist cause, he did so partly from conviction, but mostly for love of Maud. When Yeats's play *Cathleen ni Houlihan* was first performed in Dublin in 1902, she played the title role.

After the rapid decline and death of the controversial Irish leader Charles Stewart Parnell in 1891, Yeats felt that Irish political life lost its significance. The vacuum left by politics might be filled, he felt, by literature, art, poetry, drama, and legend. *The Celtic Twilight* (1893), a volume of essays, was Yeats's first effort toward this end, but progress was slow until 1898, when he met Augusta Lady Gregory, an aristocrat who was to become a playwright and his close friend.

Yeats (along with Lady Gregory and others) was one of the originators of the Irish Literary Theatre, which gave its first performance in Dublin in 1899 with Yeats's play *The Countess Cathleen*. To the end of his life Yeats remained a director of this theater, which became the Abbey Theatre in 1904. In the crucial period from 1899 to 1907, he managed the theater's affairs, encouraged its playwrights (notably John Millington Synge), and contributed many of his own plays that became part of the Abbey Theatre's repertoire.

The years from 1909 to 1914 mark a decisive change in his poetry. The otherworldly, ecstatic atmosphere of the early lyrics has cleared, and the poems in *Responsibilities: Poems and a Play* (1914) show a tightening and hardening of his verse line, a more sparse and resonant imagery, and a new directness with which Yeats confronts reality and its imperfections.

In 1917 Yeats published *The Wild Swans at Coole*. From then onward he reached and maintained the height of his achievement—a renewal of inspiration and a perfecting of technique that are almost without parallel in the history of English poetry. *The Tower* (1928), named after the castle he owned and had restored, is the work of a fully accomplished artist; in it, the experience of a lifetime is brought to perfection of form. Still, some of Yeats's greatest verse was written subsequently, appearing in *The Winding Stair* (1929). The poems in both of these works use, as their dominant subjects and symbols, the Easter Rising and the Irish civil war; Yeats's own tower; the Byzantine Empire and its mosaics; Plato, Plotinus, and Porphyry; and the author's interest in contemporary psychical research.

In 1922, on the foundation of the Irish Free State, Yeats accepted an invitation to become a member of the new Irish Senate: he served for six years. In 1923 he was awarded the Nobel Prize for Literature. Now a celebrated figure, he was indisputably one of the most significant modern poets. He died in January 1939 while abroad.

Had Yeats ceased to write at age 40, he would probably now be valued as a minor poet writing in a dying Pre-Raphaelite tradition that had drawn renewed beauty and poignancy for a time from the Celtic revival. There is no precedent in literary history for a poet who produces his greatest work between the ages of 50 and 75. Yeats's work of this period takes its strength from his long and dedicated apprenticeship to poetry; from his experiments in a wide range of forms of poetry, drama, and prose; and from his spiritual growth and his gradual acquisition of personal wisdom, which he incorporated into the framework of his own mythology.

LUIGI PIRANDELLO

(b. June 28, 1867, Agrigento, Sicily, Italy—d. Dec. 10, 1936, Rome)

Luigi Pirandello was an Italian playwright, novelist, and short-story writer who won the 1934 Nobel Prize for Literature. With his invention of the "theater within the theater" in the play *Sei personaggi in cerca d'autore* (1921; *Six Characters in Search of an Author*), he became an important innovator in modern drama.

In 1891 Pirandello gained his Doctorate in Philology for a thesis on the dialect of Agrigento. In 1894 his father arranged his marriage to Antonietta Portulano, the daughter of a business associate, a wealthy sulfur merchant. This marriage gave him financial independence, allowing him to live in Rome and to write. He had already published an early volume of verse, *Mal giocondo* (1889), which paid tribute to the poetic fashions set by Giosuè Carducci. This was followed by other volumes of verse. But his first significant works were short stories.

In 1903 a landslide shut down the sulfur mine in which his wife's and his father's capital was invested. Suddenly poor, Pirandello was forced to earn his living not only by writing but also by teaching Italian at a teacher's college in Rome. As a further result of the financial disaster, his wife developed a persecution mania, which manifested itself in a frenzied jealousy of her husband. His torment ended only with her removal to a sanatorium in 1919 (she died in 1959). It was this bitter experience that finally determined the theme of his most characteristic work, already perceptible in his early short stories—the exploration of the tightly closed world of the forever changeable human personality.

Pirandello's early narrative style stems from the *verismo* ("realism") of two Italian novelists of the late 19th century—Luigi Capuana and Giovanni Verga. Success came with his third novel, often acclaimed as his best, *Il fu Mattia Pascal* (1904; *The Late Mattia Pascal*). Although the theme is not typically "Pirandellian," since the obstacles confronting its hero result from external circumstances, it already shows the acute psychological observation that was later to be directed toward the exploration of his characters' subconscious. Other novels, notably *I vecchi e i giovani* (1913; *The Old and The Young*) and *Uno, nessuno e centomila* (1925–26; *One, None, and a Hundred Thousand*), followed.

Pirandello also wrote over 50 plays. He had first turned to the theater in 1898 with *L'epilogo*, but the accidents that prevented its production until 1910 (when it was retitled *La morsa*) kept him from other than sporadic attempts at drama until the success of *Così è (se vi pare)* in 1917. This delay may have been fortunate for the development of his dramatic powers. *L'epilogo* does not greatly differ from other drama of its period, but *Così è (se vi pare)* began the series of plays that were to make him world famous in the 1920s. Its title can be translated as *Right You Are (If You Think You Are)*. A demonstration, in dramatic terms, of the relativity of truth, and a rejection of the idea of any objective reality not at the mercy of individual vision, it anticipates Pirandello's two great plays, *Six Characters in Search of an Author* (1921) and *Enrico IV* (1922; *Henry IV*).

Six Characters is the most arresting presentation of the typical Pirandellian contrast between art, which is unchanging, and life, which is an inconstant flux. Characters that have been rejected by their author materialize on stage, throbbing with a more intense vitality than the real actors, who, inevitably, distort their drama as they attempt its presentation. And in *Henry IV* the theme is madness, which lies just under the skin of ordinary life and is, perhaps, superior to ordinary life in its construction of a satisfying reality. The play finds dramatic strength in its hero's choice of retirement into unreality in preference to life in the uncertain world. The production of *Six Characters* in Paris in 1923 made Pirandello widely known, and his work became one of the central influences on the French theater.

The universal acclaim that followed *Six Characters* and *Henry IV* sent Pirandello touring the world (1925–27) with his own company, the Teatro d'Arte in Rome. It also emboldened him to disfigure some of his later plays (e.g., *Ciascuno a suo modo* [1924]) by calling attention to himself, just as in some of the later short stories it is the surrealistic and fantastic elements that are accentuated.

After the dissolution, because of financial losses, of the Teatro d'Arte in 1928, Pirandello spent his remaining years in frequent and extensive travel. In his will he requested that there should be no public ceremony marking his death—only "a hearse of the poor, the horse and the coachman."

MARCEL PROUST

(b. July 10, 1871, Auteuil, near Paris, France—d. Nov. 18, 1922, Paris)

Marcel Proust was a French novelist and is best known as the author of *À la recherche du temps perdu* (1913–27; *In Search of Lost Time*), a seven-volume novel based on Proust's life told psychologically and allegorically.

Proust was the son of an eminent physician of provincial French Catholic descent and the daughter of a wealthy Jewish family. After a first attack in 1880, he suffered from asthma throughout his life. In 1896 he published *Les Plaisirs et les jours* (*Pleasures and Days*), a collection of short stories at once precious and profound, most of which had appeared during 1892–93 in the magazines *Le Banquet* and *La Revue Blanche*. From 1895 to 1899 he wrote *Jean Santeuil*, an autobiographical novel that showed awakening genius. A gradual disengagement from social life coincided with growing ill health and with his active involvement in the Dreyfus affair of 1897–99, when French politics and society were split by the movement to liberate the Jewish army officer Alfred Dreyfus, unjustly imprisoned on Devil's Island as a spy. Proust helped to organize petitions and assisted Dreyfus's lawyer Labori, courageously defying the risk of social ostracism.

The death of Proust's father in 1903 and of his mother in 1905 left him grief stricken and alone but financially independent and free to attempt his great novel. At least one early version was written in 1905–06. Another, begun in 1907, was laid aside in October 1908. This had itself been interrupted by a series of brilliant parodies—of Balzac, Flaubert, Renan, Saint-Simon, and others of Proust's favorite French authors—called "L'Affaire Lemoine" (published in *Le Figaro*), through which he endeavored to purge his style of extraneous influences. In January 1909 occurred the real-life incident of an involuntary revival of a childhood memory through the taste of tea and a rusk biscuit (which in his novel became madeleine cake); in July he began *À la recherche du temps perdu*.

He thought of marrying "a very young and delightful girl" whom he met at Cabourg, a seaside resort in Normandy that became the Balbec of his novel, where he spent summer holidays from 1907 to 1914. Instead, he retired from the world to write his novel, finishing the first draft in September 1912. The first volume, *Du côté de chez Swann* (*Swann's Way*), was refused by the best-selling publishers Fasquelle and Ollendorff and even by the intellectual *La Nouvelle Revue Française*, under the direction of the novelist André Gide, but was finally issued at the author's expense in November 1913 by the progressive young publisher Bernard Grasset and met with some success. Proust then planned only two further volumes, the premature appearance of which was fortunately thwarted by his anguish at the flight and death of his secretary Alfred Agostinelli and by the outbreak of World War I.

During the war he revised the remainder of his novel, enriching and deepening its feeling, texture, and construction, increasing the realistic and satirical elements, and tripling its length. In this majestic process he transformed a work that in its earlier state was still below the level of his highest powers into one of the greatest achievements of the modern novel. In June 1919 *À l'ombre des jeunes filles en fleurs* (*Within a Budding Grove*) was published simultaneously with a reprint of *Swann* and with *Pastiches et mélanges*, a miscellaneous volume containing "L'Affaire Lemoine" and other works. In December 1919, through Léon Daudet's recommendation, *À l'ombre* received the Prix Goncourt, and Proust suddenly became world famous. Three more installments appeared in his lifetime, with the benefit of his final revision, comprising *Le Côté de Guermantes* (1920–21; *The Guermantes Way*) and *Sodome et Gomorrhe* (1921–22; *Sodom and Gomorrah*).

Proust died in Paris of pneumonia, succumbing to a weakness of the lungs that many had mistaken for a form of hypochondria and struggling to the last with the revision of *La Prisonnière* (*The Captive*). The last three parts of *À la recherche* were published posthumously, in an advanced but not final stage of revision: *La Prisonnière* (1923), *Albertine disparue* (1925; *The Fugitive*), and *Le Temps retrouvé* (1927; *Time Regained*). The novel remains one of the supreme achievements of modern fiction.

ROBERT FROST

(b. March 26, 1874, San Francisco, Calif., U.S.—d. Jan. 29, 1963, Boston, Mass.)

The American poet Robert Frost was much admired for his depictions of the rural life of New England, his command of American colloquial speech, and his realistic verse portraying ordinary people in everyday situations.

Frost attended Dartmouth College and continued to labor on the poetic career he had begun in a small way during high school; he first achieved professional publication in 1894 when *The Independent*, a weekly literary journal, printed his poem *My Butterfly: An Elegy*. Impatient with academic routine, Frost left Dartmouth after less than a year and married. The young poet supported his wife, Elinor, by teaching school and farming, neither with notable success. Frost resumed his college education at Harvard University in 1897 but left after two years' study there. From 1900 to 1909 the family raised poultry on a farm near Derry, New Hampshire, and for a time Frost also taught. He became an enthusiastic botanist and acquired his poetic persona of a New England rural sage during the years he and his family spent at Derry. All this while he was writing poems, but publishing outlets showed little interest in them.

By 1911 Frost was fighting against discouragement. Poetry had always been considered a young person's game, but Frost, who was nearly 40 years old, had not published a single book of poems and had seen just a handful appear in magazines. In 1911 ownership of the Derry farm passed to Frost. A momentous decision was made: to sell the farm and use the proceeds to make a radical new start in London, where publishers were perceived to be more receptive to new talent. Accordingly, in August 1912 the Frost family sailed across the Atlantic to England. Frost carried with him sheaves of verses he had written but not gotten into print. English publishers in London did indeed prove more receptive to innovative verse, and, through his own vigorous efforts and those of the expatriate American poet Ezra Pound, Frost within a year had published *A Boy's Will* (1913). From this first book, such poems as *Storm Fear*, *Mowing*, and *The Tuft of Flowers* have remained standard anthology pieces.

A Boy's Will was followed in 1914 by a second collection, *North of Boston*, that introduced some of the most popular poems in all of Frost's work, among them *Mending Wall*, *The Death of the Hired Man*, *Home Burial*, and *After Apple-Picking*. In London, Frost's name was frequently mentioned by those who followed the course of modern literature, and soon American visitors were returning home with news of this unknown poet who was causing a sensation abroad.

The outbreak of World War I brought the Frosts back to the United States in 1915. By then the Boston poet Amy Lowell's review had already appeared in *The New Republic*, and writers and publishers throughout the Northeast were aware that a writer of unusual abilities stood in their midst. The American publishing house of Henry Holt had brought out its edition of *North of Boston* in 1914. It became a best-seller, and, by the time the Frost family landed in Boston, Holt was adding the American edition of *A Boy's Will*. Frost soon found himself besieged by magazines seeking to publish his poems. Never before had an American poet achieved such rapid fame after such a disheartening delay. From this moment his career rose on an ascending curve.

Frost bought a small farm at Franconia, New Hampshire, in 1915, but his income from both poetry and farming proved inadequate to support his family, and so he lectured and taught part-time at Amherst College and at the

University of Michigan from 1916 to 1938. Any remaining doubt about his poetic abilities was dispelled by the collection *Mountain Interval* (1916), which continued the high level established by his first books. His reputation was further enhanced by *New Hampshire* (1923), which received the Pulitzer Prize. That prize was also awarded to Frost's *Collected Poems* (1930) and to the collections *A Further Range* (1936) and *A Witness Tree* (1942). Frost served as a poet-in-residence at Harvard (1939–43), Dartmouth (1943–49), and Amherst College (1949–63), and in his old age he gathered honors and awards from every quarter. He was the poetry consultant to the Library of Congress (1958–59), and he recited his poem *The Gift Outright* at the inauguration of President John F. Kennedy in 1961.

THOMAS MANN

(b. June 6, 1875, Lübeck, Ger.—d. Aug. 12, 1955, near Zürich, Switz.)

Thomas Mann was a German novelist and essayist whose early novels—*Buddenbrooks* (1900), *Der Tod in Venedig* (1912; *Death in Venice*), and *Der Zauberberg* (1924; *The Magic Mountain*)—earned him the Nobel Prize for Literature in 1929.

After perfunctory work in Munich in an insurance office and on the editorial staff of *Simplicissimus*, a satirical weekly, Mann devoted himself to writing. His early tales, collected as *Der kleine Herr Friedemann* (1898), reflect the aestheticism of the 1890s but are given depth by the influence of the philosophers Schopenhauer and Nietzsche and the composer Wagner, to all of whom Mann was always to acknowledge a deep, if ambiguous, debt.

In his first novel, *Buddenbrooks*, Mann built the story of the family and its business house over four generations, showing how an artistic streak not only unfits the family's later members for the practicalities of business life but undermines their vitality as well. But, almost against his will, Mann also wrote a tender elegy for the old bourgeois virtues.

The outbreak of World War I evoked Mann's ardent patriotism and awoke, too, an awareness of the artist's social commitment. In 1918 he published a large political treatise, *Reflections of an Unpolitical Man*, in which all his ingenuity of mind was summoned to justify the authoritarian state as against democracy, creative irrationalism as against "flat" rationalism, and inward culture as against moralistic civilization. This work belongs to the tradition of "revolutionary conservatism" that leads from the 19th-century German nationalistic and antidemocratic thinkers Paul Anton de Lagarde and Houston Stewart Chamberlain, the apostle of the superiority of the "Germanic" race, toward National Socialism; and Mann later was to repudiate these ideas.

With the establishment of the German (Weimar) Republic in 1919, Mann slowly revised his outlook. His new position was clarified in the novel *The Magic Mountain*. Its theme grows out of an earlier motif: a young engineer, Hans Castorp, visiting a cousin in a sanatorium in Davos, abandons practical life to submit to the rich seductions of disease, inwardness, and death. But the sanatorium comes to be the spiritual reflection of the possibilities and dangers of the actual world. In the end, somewhat skeptically but humanely, Castorp decides for life and service to his people.

From this time onward Mann's imaginative effort was directed to the novel. His literary and cultural essays began to play an ever-growing part in elucidating and communicating his awareness of the fragility of humaneness, tolerance, and reason in the face of political crisis. In 1930 he gave a courageous address in Berlin, "Ein Appell an die Vernunft" ("An Appeal to Reason"), appealing for the formation of a common front of the cultured bourgeoisie and the socialist working class against the inhuman fanaticism of the National Socialists. In essays and on lecture tours in Germany, to Paris, Vienna, Warsaw, Amsterdam, and elsewhere during the 1930s, Mann, while steadfastly attacking Nazi policy, often expressed sympathy with socialist and communist principles in the very general sense that they were the guarantee of humanism and freedom.

When Hitler became chancellor early in 1933, Mann and his wife, on holiday in Switzerland, were warned by their son and daughter in Munich not to return. For some years his home was in Switzerland, near Zürich, but he traveled widely, visiting the United States on lecture tours and finally, in 1938, settling there. In 1936 he was deprived of his German citizenship; in the same year the University of Bonn took away the honorary doctorate it had bestowed in 1919 (it was restored in 1949). From 1936 to 1944 Mann was a citizen of Czechoslovakia. In 1944 he became a U.S. citizen. After the war, he refused to return to Germany to live. In 1952 he settled again near Zürich.

The novels on which Mann was working throughout this period of exile reflect variously the cultural crisis of his times. In *Doktor Faustus*, begun in 1943 at the darkest period of the war, Mann wrote the most directly political of his novels. It is the life story of a German composer, Adrian Leverkühn, born in 1885, who dies in 1940 after 10 years of mental alienation. A solitary, estranged figure, he "speaks" the experience of his times in his music, and the story of Leverkühn's compositions is that of German culture in the two decades before 1930—more specifically of the collapse of traditional humanism and the victory of the mixture of sophisticated nihilism and barbaric primitivism that undermine it.

The composition of the novel was fully documented

by Mann in 1949 in *The Genesis of a Novel. Doktor Faustus* exhausted him as no other work of his had done, and *The Holy Sinner* and *The Black Swan*, published in 1951 and 1953, respectively, show a relaxation of intensity in spite of their accomplished, even virtuoso style.

Mann's style is finely wrought and full of resources, enriched by humor, irony, and parody; his composition is subtle and many-layered, brilliantly realistic on one level and yet reaching to deeper levels of symbolism.

LU XUN

(b. Sept. 25, 1881, Shaoxing, Zhejiang province, China—d. Oct. 19, 1936, Shanghai)

Lu Xun, which is the pen name of Zhou Shuren, was a Chinese writer commonly considered the greatest in 20th-century Chinese literature. He was also an important critic known for his sharp and unique essays on the historical traditions and modern conditions of China.

Born to a family that was traditional, wealthy, and esteemed (his grandfather had been a government official in Beijing), Zhou Shuren had a happy childhood. In 1893, however, his grandfather was sentenced to prison for examination fraud, and his father became bedridden. The family's reputation declined, and they were treated with disdain by their community and relatives. This experience is thought to have had a great influence on his writing, which was marked by sensitivity and pessimism.

Zhou Shuren left his hometown in 1899 and attended a mining school in Nanjing; there he developed an interest in Darwin's theory of evolution, which became an important influence in his work. Chinese intellectuals of the time understood Darwin's theory to encourage the struggle for social reform, to privilege the new and fresh over the old and traditional. In 1902 he traveled to Japan to study Japanese and medical science, and while there he became a supporter of the Chinese revolutionaries who gathered there. In 1903 he began to write articles for radical magazines edited by Chinese students in Japan. In 1905 he entered an arranged marriage against his will. In 1909 he published, with his younger brother Zhou Zuoren, a two-volume translation of 19th-century European stories, in the hope that it would inspire readers to revolution, but the project failed to attract interest. Disillusioned, Lu Xun returned to China later that year.

After working for several years as a teacher in his hometown and then as a low-level government official in Beijing, Lu Xun returned to writing and became associated with the nascent Chinese literary movement in 1918. That year, at the urging of friends, he published his now-famous short story *Kuangren riji* ("Diary of a Madman"). Modeled on the Russian realist Nikolay Gogol's tale of the same title, the story is a condemnation of traditional Confucian culture, which the madman narrator sees as a "man-eating" society. The first published Western-style story written wholly in vernacular Chinese, it was a tour de force that attracted immediate attention and helped gain acceptance for the short-story form as an effective literary vehicle.

Another representative work is the novelette *A-Q zhengzhuan* (1921; *The True Story of Ah Q*). A mixture of humor and pathos, it is a repudiation of the old order; it added "Ah Q-ism" to the modern Chinese language as a term characterizing the Chinese penchant for rationalizing defeat as a "spiritual victory." These stories, which were collected in *Nahan* (1923; *Call to Arms*), established Lu Xun's reputation as the leading Chinese writer. Three years later the collection *Panghuang* (1926; *Wandering*) was published. His various symbolic prose poems, which were published in the collection *Yecao* (1927; *Wild Grass*), as well as his reminiscences and retold classical tales, all reveal a modern sensibility informed by sardonic humor and biting satire.

In the 1920s Lu Xun worked at various universities in Beijing as a part-time professor of Chinese script and literature. His academic study *Zhongguo xiaoshuo shilue* (1923–24; *A Brief History of Chinese Fiction*) and companion compilations of classical fiction remain standard works. His translations, especially those of Russian works, are also considered significant.

Despite his success, Lu Xun continued to struggle with his increasingly pessimistic view of Chinese society, which was aggravated by conflicts in his personal and professional life. In addition to marital troubles and mounting pressures from the government, his disagreements with Zhou Zuoren (who had also become one of the leading intellectuals in Beijing) led to a rift between the two brothers in 1926. Such depressing conditions led Lu Xun to formulate the idea that one could resist social darkness only when he was pessimistic about the society. His famous phrase "resistance of despair" is commonly considered a core concept of his thought.

Forced by these political and personal circumstances to flee Beijing in 1926, Lu Xun traveled to Xiamen and Guangzhou, finally settling in Shanghai in 1927. There he began to live with Xu Guangping, his former student; they had a son in 1929. Lu Xun stopped writing fiction and devoted himself to writing satiric critical essays (*zawen*), which he used as a form of political protest. In 1930 he became the nominal leader of the League of Left-Wing Writers. During the following decade he began to see the Chinese communists as the only salvation for his country. Although he himself refused to join the Chinese Communist Party, he considered himself a *tongluren* (fellow traveler), recruiting many writers and countrymen to the communist cause through his Chinese translations of Marxist literary theories, as well as through his own political writing.

During the last several years of Lu Xun's life, the government prohibited the publication of most of his work, so he published the majority of his new articles under various pseudonyms. He criticized the Shanghai communist literary circles for their embrace of propaganda, and he was politically attacked by many of their members. In 1934 he described his political position as *hengzhan* ("horizontal stand"), meaning he was struggling simultaneously against both the right and the left, against both cultural conservatism and mechanical evolution. *Hengzhan*, the most important idea in Lu Xun's later thought, indicates the complex and tragic predicament of an intellectual in modern society.

The Chinese communist movement adopted Lu Xun posthumously as the exemplar of Socialist Realism. Many of his fiction and prose works have been incorporated into school textbooks. In 1951 the Lu Xun Museum opened in Shanghai; it contains letters, manuscripts, photographs, and other memorabilia. English translations of Lu Xun's works include *Silent China: Selected Writings of Lu Xun* (1973), *Lu Hsun: Complete Poems* (1988), and *Diary of a Madman and Other Stories* (1990).

VIRGINIA WOOLF

(b. Jan. 25, 1882, London, Eng.—d. March 28, 1941, near Rodmell, Sussex)

Virginia Woolf was an English writer whose novels, through their nonlinear approaches to narrative, exerted a major influence on the genre. While she is best known for her novels, especially *Mrs. Dalloway* (1925) and *To the Lighthouse* (1927), Woolf also wrote pioneering essays on artistic theory, literary history, women's writing, and the politics of power.

Early Life and Influences

Born Virginia Stephen, she was the child of ideal Victorian parents. Her father, Leslie Stephen, was an eminent literary figure and the first editor (1882–91) of the *Dictionary of National Biography*. Her mother, Julia Jackson, possessed great beauty and a reputation for saintly self-sacrifice. Both Julia Jackson's first husband, Herbert Duckworth, and Leslie's first wife, a daughter of the novelist William Makepeace Thackeray, had died unexpectedly, leaving her three children and him one. Julia Jackson Duckworth and Leslie Stephen married in 1878, and four children followed: Vanessa (born 1879), Thoby (born 1880), Virginia (born 1882), and Adrian (born 1883).

The Stephen family made summer migrations from London to the rugged Cornwall coast. That annual relocation cleanly structured Woolf's childhood world. Her neatly divided, predictable world ended, however, when her mother died in 1895 at age 49. Woolf was just emerging from depression when, in 1897, her half sister Stella Duckworth died at age 28. Then in 1904, after her father died, she had a nervous breakdown.

While she was recovering, Vanessa supervised the Stephen children's move to the bohemian Bloomsbury section of London. Leonard Woolf dined with them in November 1904, just before sailing to Ceylon (now Sri Lanka) to become a colonial administrator. Soon the Stephens hosted weekly gatherings of radical young people. Then, after a family excursion to Greece in 1906, Thoby died of typhoid fever. Virginia Woolf grieved but did not slip into depression. She overcame the loss of

This photograph of the influential novelist Virginia Woolf was taken in 1902.

Thoby and the "loss" of Vanessa, who became engaged to Clive Bell just after Thoby's death, through writing. Vanessa's marriage (and perhaps Thoby's absence) helped transform conversation at the avant-garde gatherings of what came to be known as the Bloomsbury group into irreverent repartee that inspired Woolf to exercise her wit publicly, even while privately she was writing her poignant *Reminiscences*—about her childhood and her lost mother—which was published in 1908.

Early Fiction

Woolf determined in 1908 to "re-form" the novel. While writing anonymous reviews for the *Times Literary Supplement* and other journals, she experimented with such a novel, which she called *Melymbrosia*. In the summer of 1911, Leonard Woolf returned from the East. After he resigned from the colonial service, Leonard and Virginia married in August 1912.

Between 1910 and 1915, Virginia Woolf's mental health was precarious. Nevertheless, she completely recast *Melymbrosia* as *The Voyage Out* in 1913. Rachel Vinrace, the novel's central character, is a sheltered young woman who, on an excursion to South America, is introduced to freedom and sexuality. After an excursion up the Amazon, Rachel contracts a terrible illness that plunges her into delirium and then death. The book endorses no explanation for her death. That indeterminacy set the book at odds with the certainties of the Victorian era and especially the conventions of realism.

Woolf's manic-depressive worries provoked a suicide attempt in September 1913. Publication of *The Voyage Out* was delayed until early 1915. That April, she sank into a distressed state in which she was often delirious. Later that year she overcame the "vile imaginations" that had threatened her sanity. She kept the demons of mania and depression mostly at bay for the rest of her life.

In 1917 the Woolfs bought a printing press and founded the Hogarth Press, named for Hogarth House, their home in the London suburbs. The Woolfs themselves (she was the compositor while he worked the press) published their own *Two Stories* in the summer of 1917. It consisted of Leonard's *Three Jews* and Virginia's *The Mark on the Wall*, the latter about contemplation itself.

Proving that she could master the traditional form of the novel before breaking it, Woolf plotted her next novel in two romantic triangles, with its protagonist Katharine in both. *Night and Day* (1919) focuses on the very sort of details that Woolf had deleted from *The Voyage Out*: credible dialogue, realistic descriptions of early 20th-century settings, and investigations of issues such as class, politics, and suffrage.

Woolf was writing nearly a review a week for the *Times Literary Supplement* in 1918. Her essay *Modern Novels* (1919; revised in 1925 as *Modern Fiction*) attacked the "materialists" who wrote about superficial rather than spiritual or "luminous" experiences. The Woolfs also printed by hand, with Vanessa Bell's illustrations, Virginia's *Kew Gardens* (1919), a story organized, like a Post-Impressionistic painting, by pattern. With the Hogarth Press's emergence as a major publishing house, the Woolfs gradually ceased being their own printers. In 1919 they bought a cottage in Rodmell village called Monk's House, which looked out over the Sussex Downs and the meadows where the River Ouse wound down to the English Channel. Three years later Woolf published *Jacob's Room*, in which she transformed personal grief over the death of Thoby Stephen into a "spiritual shape." Though *Jacob's Room* is an antiwar novel, Woolf feared that she had ventured too far beyond representation.

Major Period

At the beginning of 1924, the Woolfs moved their city residence from the suburbs back to Bloomsbury, where they were less isolated from London society. Soon the aristocratic Vita Sackville-West began to court Woolf, a relationship that would blossom into a lesbian affair.

Having already written a story about a Mrs. Dalloway, Woolf thought of a foiling device that would pair that highly sensitive woman with a shell-shocked war victim, a Mr. Smith, so that "the sane and the insane" would exist "side by side." Her aim was to "tunnel" into these two characters until Clarissa Dalloway's affirmations meet Septimus Smith's negations. In *Mrs. Dalloway* (1925), the boorish doctors presume to understand personality, but its essence evades them. This novel is as patterned as a Post-Impressionist painting but is also so accurately representational that the reader can trace Clarissa's and Septimus's movements through the streets of London on a single day in June 1923. At the end of the day, Clarissa gives a grand party and Septimus commits suicide. Their lives come together when the doctor who was treating (or, rather, mistreating) Septimus arrives at Clarissa's party with news of the death. The main characters are connected by motifs and, finally, by Clarissa's intuiting why Septimus threw his life away.

Woolf wished to build on her achievement in *Mrs. Dalloway* by merging the novelistic and elegiac forms. As an elegy, *To the Lighthouse*—published on May 5, 1927, the 32nd anniversary of Julia Stephen's death—evoked her childhood summers. As a novel, it broke narrative continuity into a tripartite structure and thereby melded into its structure questions about creativity and the nature and function of art.

Their relationship having cooled by 1927, Woolf sought

to reclaim Sackville-West through a "biography" that would include Sackville family history. She solved biographical, historical, and personal dilemmas with the story of Orlando, who lives from Elizabethan times through the entire 18th century; he then becomes female, experiences debilitating gender constraints, and lives into the 20th century. Woolf herself writes in mock-heroic imitation of biographical styles that change over the same period of time. Thus, *Orlando: A Biography* (1928) exposes the artificiality of both gender and genre prescriptions.

In 1921 John Maynard Keynes had told Woolf that one of her memoirs represented her best writing. Afterward she was increasingly angered by masculine condescension to female talent. In *A Room of One's Own* (1929), Woolf blamed women's absence from history not on their lack of brains and talent but on their poverty. For her 1931 talk *Professions for Women*, Woolf studied the history of women's education and employment and argued that unequal opportunities for women negatively affect all of society.

Having praised a 1930 exhibit of Vanessa Bell's paintings for their wordlessness, Woolf planned a mystical novel that would be similarly impersonal and abstract. In *The Waves* (1931), poetic interludes describe the sea and sky from dawn to dusk. *The Waves* offers a six-sided shape that illustrates how each individual experiences events uniquely. Through *To the Lighthouse* and *The Waves*, Woolf became, with James Joyce and William Faulkner, one of the three major English-language Modernist experimenters in stream-of-consciousness writing.

LATE WORK

Even before finishing *The Waves*, she began compiling a scrapbook of clippings illustrating the horrors of war, the threat of fascism, and the oppression of women. The discrimination against women that Woolf had discussed in *A Room of One's Own* and *Professions for Women* inspired her to plan a book that would trace the story of a fictional family named Pargiter and explain the social conditions affecting family members over a period of time. In *The Pargiters: A Novel-Essay* she would alternate between sections of fiction and of fact. The task of doing so, however, was daunting.

Woolf took a holiday from *The Pargiters* to write a mock biography of Flush, the dog of poet Elizabeth Barrett Browning. *Flush* (1933) remains both a biographical satire and a lighthearted exploration of perception, in this case a dog's. But she feared she would never finish *The Pargiters*. She solved this dilemma by jettisoning the essay sections, keeping the family narrative, and renaming her book *The Years*. She narrated 50 years of family history through the decline of class and patriarchal systems, the rise of feminism, and the threat of another war. Though (or perhaps because) Woolf's trimming muted the book's radicalism, *The Years* (1937) became a best-seller.

Woolf's chief anodyne against Adolf Hitler, World War II, and her own despair was writing. During the bombing of London in 1940 and 1941, she worked on *Between the Acts*. In her novel, war threatens art and humanity itself. Despite *Between the Acts*' affirmation of the value of art, Woolf worried that this novel was "too slight" and indeed that all writing was irrelevant when England seemed on the verge of invasion and civilization about to slide over a precipice. Facing such horrors, a depressed Woolf found herself unable to write. On March 28, 1941, she walked behind Monk's House and down to the River Ouse, put stones in her pockets, and drowned herself. *Between the Acts* was published posthumously later that year.

JAMES JOYCE

(b. Feb. 2, 1882, Dublin, Ire.—d. Jan. 13, 1941, Zürich, Switz.)

James Joyce was an Irish novelist noted for his experimental use of language and exploration of new literary methods in such large works of fiction as *Ulysses* (1922) and *Finnegans Wake* (1939).

Joyce was educated at University College, Dublin, which was then staffed by Jesuit priests. There he studied languages and reserved his energies for extracurricular activities, reading widely—particularly in books not recommended by the Jesuits—and taking an active part in the college's Literary and Historical Society. Early success in publishing a theater review confirmed Joyce in his resolution to become a writer and persuaded his family, friends, and teachers that the resolution was justified. He received a B.A. in 1902. To support himself while writing, he decided to become a doctor, but, after attending a few lectures in Dublin, he borrowed what money he could and went to Paris, where he abandoned the idea of medical studies, wrote some book reviews, and studied in the Sainte-Geneviève Library.

By 1903 he had begun writing a lengthy naturalistic novel, *Stephen Hero*, based on the events of his own life, when in 1904 George Russell offered £1 each for some simple short stories with an Irish background to appear in a farmers' magazine, *The Irish Homestead*. In response Joyce began writing the stories published as *Dubliners* (1914). Three stories, *The Sisters*, *Eveline*, and *After the Race*, had appeared under the pseudonym Stephen Dedalus before the editor decided that Joyce's work was not suitable for his readers. Meanwhile Joyce had met a girl named Nora Barnacle, with whom he fell in love on June 16, the day that he chose as what is known as "Bloomsday" (the day of his novel *Ulysses*). Eventually he persuaded her to leave Ireland with him, although he refused, on principle, to go through a ceremony of marriage.

Joyce and Barnacle left Dublin together in October 1904. Joyce obtained a position in the Berlitz School, Pola, Austria-Hungary, working in his spare time at his novel and short stories. In 1905 they moved to Trieste. In 1906–07, for eight months, he worked at a bank in Rome, disliking almost everything he saw. His studies in European literature had interested him in both the Symbolists and the Realists; his work began to show a synthesis of these two rival movements. He decided that *Stephen Hero* lacked artistic control and form and rewrote it as "a work in five chapters" under a title—*A Portrait of the Artist as a Young Man*—intended to direct attention to its focus upon the central figure.

After the outbreak of World War I, Joyce's financial difficulties were great. He was helped by a large grant from Edith Rockefeller McCormick and finally by a series of grants from Harriet Shaw Weaver, editor of the *Egoist* magazine, which by 1930 had amounted to more than £23,000. Her generosity resulted partly from her admiration for his work and partly from her sympathy with his difficulties, for, as well as poverty, he had to contend with eye diseases that never really left him. From February 1917 until 1930 he endured a series of 25 operations for iritis, glaucoma, and cataracts, sometimes being for short intervals totally blind. Despite this he kept up his spirits and continued working, some of his most joyful passages being composed when his health was at its worst.

Unable to find an English printer willing to set up *A Portrait of the Artist as a Young Man* for book publication, Weaver published it herself, having the sheets printed in the United States, where it was also published in 1916.

Encouraged by the acclaim given to this, in March 1918, the American *Little Review* began to publish episodes from *Ulysses*, continuing until the work was banned in December 1920. An autobiographical novel, *A Portrait of the Artist* traces the intellectual and emotional development of a young man named Stephen Dedalus and ends with his decision to leave Dublin for Paris to devote his life to art.

After World War I, Joyce returned for a few months to Trieste, and then, at the invitation of Ezra Pound, he went to Paris in July 1920. His novel *Ulysses* was published there on Feb. 2, 1922, by Sylvia Beach, proprietor of a bookshop called Shakespeare and Company. Already well known because of the censorship troubles, it became immediately famous upon publication. *Ulysses* is constructed as a modern parallel to Homer's *Odyssey*. All of the action of the novel takes place in Dublin on a single day (June 16, 1904). The three central characters—Stephen Dedalus (the hero of Joyce's earlier *Portrait of the Artist*); Leopold Bloom, a Jewish advertising canvasser; and his wife, Molly Bloom—are intended to be modern counterparts of Telemachus, Ulysses, and Penelope. By the use of interior monologue Joyce reveals the innermost thoughts and feelings of these characters as they live hour by hour, passing from a public bath to a funeral, library, maternity hospital, and brothel.

In Paris Joyce worked on *Finnegans Wake*, the title of which was kept secret, the novel being known simply as "Work in Progress" until it was published in its entirety in May 1939. In addition to his chronic eye troubles, Joyce suffered great and prolonged anxiety over his daughter's mental health. What had seemed her slight eccentricity grew into unmistakable and sometimes violent mental disorder that Joyce tried by every possible means to cure, but it became necessary finally to place her in a mental hospital near Paris. In 1931 he and Barnacle visited London, where they were married, his scruples on this point having yielded to his daughter's complaints.

Meanwhile he wrote and rewrote sections of *Finnegans Wake*; often a passage was revised more than a dozen times before he was satisfied. Basically the book is, in one sense, the story of a publican in Chapelizod, near Dublin, his wife, and their three children; but Mr. Humphrey Chimpden Earwicker (often designated by variations on his initials, HCE, one form of which is "Here Comes Everybody"), Mrs. Anna Livia Plurabelle, Kevin, Jerry, and Isabel are every family of mankind, the archetypal family about whom all humanity is dreaming. It is thousands of dreams in one. Languages merge: Anna Livia has "vlossyhair"—*włosy* being Polish for "hair"; "a bad of wind" blows, *bâd* being Turkish for "wind." Characters from literature and history appear and merge and disappear as "the intermisunderstanding minds of the anticollaborators" dream on. And throughout the book Joyce himself is present, joking, mocking his critics, defending his theories, remembering his father, enjoying himself.

After the fall of France in World War II (1940), Joyce took his family back to Zürich, where he died, still disappointed with the reception given to his last book.

FRANZ KAFKA

(b. July 3, 1883, Prague, Bohemia, Austria-Hungary [now in Czech Republic]—d. June 3, 1924, Kierling, near Vienna, Austria)

Franz Kafka was a German-language writer of visionary fiction, whose posthumously published novels—especially *Der Prozess* (1925; *The Trial*) and *Das Schloss* (1926; *The Castle*)—express the anxieties and alienation of 20th-century humankind.

The son of an assimilated Jew who held only perfunctorily to the religious practices and social formalities of the Jewish community, Kafka was German both in language and culture. He was a timid, guilt-ridden, and obedient child who did well in elementary school and in the Altstädter Staatsgymnasium, an exacting high school for the academic elite. He was respected and liked by his teachers. Inwardly, however, he rebelled against the authoritarian institution and the dehumanized humanistic curriculum, with its emphasis on rote learning and classical languages.

Kafka's opposition to established society became apparent when, as an adolescent, he declared himself a socialist as well as an atheist. Throughout his adult life he expressed qualified sympathies for the socialists, he attended meetings of the Czech Anarchists (before World War I), and in his later years he showed marked interest and sympathy for a socialized Zionism. Even then he was essentially passive and politically unengaged. As a Jew, Kafka was isolated from the German community in Prague, but, as a modern intellectual, he was also alienated from his own Jewish heritage. He was sympathetic to Czech political and cultural aspirations, but his identification with German culture kept even these sympathies subdued. Thus, social isolation and rootlessness contributed to Kafka's lifelong personal unhappiness. Kafka did, however, become friendly with some German-Jewish intellectuals and literati in Prague, and in 1902 he met Max Brod; this minor literary artist became the most intimate and solicitous of Kafka's friends, and eventually he emerged as the promoter, savior, and interpreter of Kafka's writings and as his most influential biographer.

The two men became acquainted while Kafka was

studying law at the University of Prague. He received his doctorate in 1906, and in 1907 he took up regular employment with an insurance company. The long hours and exacting requirements of the Assicurazioni Generali, however, did not permit Kafka to devote himself to writing. In 1908 he found in Prague a job in the seminationalized Workers' Accident Insurance Institute for the Kingdom of Bohemia. There he remained until 1917, when tuberculosis forced him to take intermittent sick leaves and, finally, to retire (with a pension) in 1922, about two years before he died. In his job he was considered tireless and ambitious; he soon became the right hand of his boss, and he was esteemed and liked by all who worked with him.

Generally speaking, Kafka was a charming, intelligent, and humorous individual, but he found his routine office job and the exhausting double life into which it forced him (for his nights were frequently consumed in writing) to be excruciating torture, and his deeper personal relationships were neurotically disturbed. The conflicting inclinations of his complex and ambivalent personality found expression in his sexual relationships. His health was poor and office work exhausted him. In 1917 he was diagnosed as having tuberculosis, and from then onward he spent frequent periods in sanatoriums.

In 1923 Kafka went to Berlin to devote himself to writing. During a vacation on the Baltic coast later that year, he met Dora Dymant (Diamant), a young Jewish socialist. The couple lived in Berlin until Kafka's health significantly worsened during the spring of 1924. After a brief final stay in Prague, where Dymant joined him, he died of tuberculosis in a clinic near Vienna.

Sought out by leading avant-garde publishers, Kafka reluctantly published a few of his writings during his lifetime. These publications include, among others, works representative of Kafka's maturity as an artist—*The*

Judgment, a long story written in 1912; two further long stories, *Die Verwandlung* (1915; *Metamorphosis*) and *In der Strafkolonie* (1919; *In the Penal Colony*); and a collection of short prose, *Ein Landarzt* (1919; *A Country Doctor*). *Ein Hungerkünstler* (1924; *A Hunger Artist*), four stories exhibiting the concision and lucidity characteristic of Kafka's late style, had been prepared by the author but did not appear until after his death.

In fact, misgivings about his work caused Kafka before his death to request that all of his unpublished manuscripts be destroyed; his literary executor, Max Brod, disregarded his instructions. Brod published the novels *The Trial*, *The Castle*, and *Amerika* in 1925, 1926, and 1927, respectively, and a collection of shorter pieces, *Beim Bau der chinesischen Mauer* (*The Great Wall of China*), in 1931.

Many of Kafka's fables contain an inscrutable, baffling mixture of the normal and the fantastic, though occasionally the strangeness may be understood as the outcome of a literary or verbal device, as when the delusions of a pathological state are given the status of reality or when the metaphor of a common figure of speech is taken literally. Thus in *The Judgment* a son unquestioningly commits suicide at the behest of his aged father. In *The Metamorphosis* the son wakes up to find himself transformed into a monstrous and repulsive insect; he slowly dies, not only because of his family's shame and its neglect of him but because of his own guilty despair.

Many of the tales are even more unfathomable. *In the Penal Colony* presents an officer who demonstrates his devotion to duty by submitting himself to the appalling (and clinically described) mutilations of his own instrument of torture. This theme, the ambiguity of a task's value and the horror of devotion to it—one of Kafka's constant preoccupations—appears again in *A Hunger Artist*. Many of the motifs in the short fables also recur in the novels.

This statue in honor of Franz Kafka was created by the artist David Cerny.

Kafka's stories and novels have provoked a wealth of interpretations. Brod and Kafka's foremost English translators, Willa and Edwin Muir, viewed the novels as allegories of divine grace. Existentialists have seen Kafka's environment of guilt and despair as the ground upon which to construct an authentic existence. Some have seen his neurotic involvement with his father as the heart of his work; others have emphasized the social criticism, the inhumanity of the powerful and their agents, the violence and barbarity that lurk beneath normal routine. Some have found an imaginative anticipation of totalitarianism in the random and faceless bureaucratic terror of *The Trial*. There is evidence in both the works and the diaries for each of these interpretations, but Kafka's work as a whole transcends them all.

T. S. ELIOT

(b. Sept. 26, 1888, St. Louis, Mo., U.S.—d. Jan. 4, 1965, London, Eng.)

Thomas Sterns Eliot was an American-English poet, playwright, literary critic, and editor who was a leader of the Modernist movement in poetry in such works as *The Waste Land* (1922) and *Four Quartets* (1943). His experiments in diction, style, and versification revitalized English poetry, and in a series of critical essays he shattered old orthodoxies and erected new ones. In 1948 he was awarded both the Order of Merit and the Nobel Prize for Literature.

Eliot entered Harvard in 1906 and received a B.A. in 1909. He spent the year 1910–11 in France, attending Henri Bergson's lectures in philosophy at the Sorbonne and reading poetry with Alain-Fournier. From 1911 to 1914 he was back at Harvard reading Indian philosophy and studying Sanskrit. By 1916 he had finished, in Europe, a dissertation entitled *Knowledge and Experience in the Philosophy of F.H.*

Bradley. But World War I had intervened, and he never returned to Harvard to take the final oral examination for the Ph.D. degree.

Eliot was to pursue four careers: editor, dramatist, literary critic, and philosophical poet. His first important publication, and the first masterpiece of "Modernism" in English, was *The Love Song of J. Alfred Prufrock*. It represented a break with the immediate past as radical as that of Samuel Taylor Coleridge and William Wordsworth in *Lyrical Ballads* (1798). From the appearance of Eliot's first volume, *Prufrock and Other Observations*, in 1917, one may conveniently date the maturity of the 20th-century poetic revolution.

For a year Eliot taught French and Latin at the Highgate School; in 1917 he began his brief career as a bank clerk in Lloyds Bank Ltd. Meanwhile he was also a prolific reviewer and essayist in both literary criticism and technical philosophy. In 1919 he published *Poems*, which contained the poem *Gerontion*, a meditative interior monologue in blank verse: nothing like this poem had appeared in English.

With the publication in 1922 of his poem *The Waste Land*, Eliot won an international reputation. *The Waste Land* expresses with great power the disenchantment, disillusionment, and disgust of the period after World War I. In a series of vignettes, loosely linked by the legend of the search for the Grail, it portrays a sterile world of panicky fears and barren lusts, and of human beings waiting for some sign or promise of redemption. *The Waste Land* showed him to be, in addition, a metrist of great virtuosity, capable of astonishing modulations ranging from the sublime to the conversational.

Consciously intended or not, Eliot's criticism created an atmosphere in which his own poetry could be better understood and appreciated than if it had to appear in a literary milieu dominated by the standards of the preceding age. In the essay *Tradition and the Individual Talent*, appearing in his first critical volume, *The Sacred Wood* (1920), Eliot asserts that tradition, as used by the poet, is not a mere repetition of the work of the immediate past; rather, it comprises the whole of European literature from Homer to the present. The poet writing in English may therefore make his own tradition by using materials from any past period, in any language.

Two other essays almost complete the Eliot critical canon: *The Metaphysical Poets* and *Andrew Marvell*, published in *Selected Essays, 1917–32* (1932). In these essays he effects a new historical perspective on the hierarchy of English poetry, putting at the top Donne and other Metaphysical poets of the 17th century and lowering poets of the 18th and 19th centuries.

Eliot was confirmed in the Church of England (1927); in that year he also became a British subject. The first long poem after his conversion was *Ash Wednesday* (1930), a religious meditation in a style entirely different from that of any of the earlier poems. This and subsequent poems were written in a more relaxed, musical, and meditative style than his earlier works.

Eliot's masterpiece is *Four Quartets*, which was issued as a book in 1943. This work made a deep impression on the reading public, and even those who were unable to accept the poems' Christian beliefs recognized the intellectual integrity with which Eliot pursued his high theme, the originality of the form he had devised, and the technical mastery of his verse. This work led to the award to Eliot, in 1948, of the Nobel Prize for Literature.

Eliot's plays, which begin with *Sweeney Agonistes* (published 1926; first performed in 1934) and end with *The Elder Statesman* (first performed 1958; published 1959), are, with the exception of *Murder in the Cathedral* (published and performed 1935), inferior to the lyric and meditative poetry. All his plays are in a blank verse of his own invention; thus he brought "poetic drama" back to the popular stage. *The Family Reunion* (1939) and *Murder in the Cathedral* are Christian tragedies, the former a tragedy of revenge, the latter of the sin of pride. *Murder in the Cathedral* is a modern miracle play on the martyrdom of Thomas Becket.

After World War II, Eliot returned to writing plays with several comedies derived from Greek drama. Eliot's career as editor was ancillary to his main interests, but his quarterly review, *The Criterion* (1922–39), was the most distinguished international critical journal of the period. He was a "director," or working editor, of the publishing firm of Faber & Faber Ltd. from the early 1920s until his death.

From the 1920s onward, Eliot's influence as a poet and as a critic—in both Great Britain and the United States—was immense. Since his death, interpreters have been markedly more critical, focusing on his complex relationship to his American origins, his elitist cultural and social views, and his exclusivist notions of tradition and of race.

EUGENE O'NEILL

(b. Oct. 16, 1888, New York, N.Y., U.S.—d. Nov. 27, 1953, Boston, Mass.)

Eugene O'Neill was a foremost American dramatist of the 20th century and the winner of the Nobel Prize for Literature in 1936.

O'Neill, who was born in a hotel and whose father was a touring actor, spent his early childhood in hotel rooms, on trains, and backstage. He was educated at boarding schools, and he attended Princeton University for one year (1906–07), after which he left school to begin what he later regarded as his real education in "life experience." He shipped to sea, lived a derelict's existence on the waterfronts of Buenos Aires, Liverpool, and New York City, submerged himself in alcohol, and attempted suicide. Recovering briefly at the age of 24, he held a job for a few months as a reporter and contributor to the poetry column of the *New London Telegraph* but soon came down with tuberculosis. Confined to the Gaylord Farm Sanitarium in Wallingford, Conn., for six months (1912–13), he confronted himself soberly and nakedly for the first time and seized the chance for what he later called his "rebirth." He began to write plays.

O'Neill's first appearance as a playwright came in the summer of 1916, in the quiet fishing village of Provincetown, Mass., where a group of young writers and painters had launched an experimental theater. In their tiny, ramshackle playhouse on a wharf, they produced his one-act sea play *Bound East for Cardiff.* The talent inherent in the play was immediately evident to the group, which that fall formed the Playwrights' Theater in Greenwich Village. Their first bill, on Nov. 3, 1916, included *Bound East for Cardiff*—O'Neill's New York debut. Although he was only one of several writers whose plays were produced by the Playwrights' Theater, his contribution within the next few years made the group's reputation. By the time his first full-length play, *Beyond the Horizon*, was produced on Broadway, Feb. 2, 1920, at the Morosco Theater, the young playwright already had a small reputation.

Beyond the Horizon impressed the critics with its tragic realism, won for O'Neill the first of four Pulitzer prizes in drama—others were for *Anna Christie*, *Strange Interlude*, and *Long Day's Journey into Night*—and brought him to the attention of a wider theater public. For the next 20 years his reputation grew steadily, both in the United States and abroad; after Shakespeare and Shaw, O'Neill became the most widely translated and produced dramatist.

O'Neill's capacity for and commitment to work were staggering. Between 1920 and 1943 he completed 20 long plays—several of them double and triple length—and a number of shorter ones. He wrote and rewrote many of his manuscripts half a dozen times before he was satisfied. His most-distinguished short plays include the four early sea plays, *Bound East for Cardiff*, *In the Zone*, *The Long Voyage Home*, and *The Moon of the Caribbees*, which were written between 1913 and 1917 and produced in 1924 under the overall title *S.S. Glencairn*; *The Emperor Jones* (1920; about the disintegration of a Pullman porter turned tropical-island dictator); and *The Hairy Ape* (1922; about the disintegration of a displaced steamship coal stoker). *Desire Under the Elms* (1924), *The Great God Brown* (1926), *Strange Interlude* (1928), *Mourning Becomes Electra* (1931), and *The Iceman Cometh* (1946) are among his important long plays. *Ah, Wilderness!* (1933) was his only comedy.

O'Neill's plays were written from an intensely personal point of view, deriving directly from the scarring effects of his family's tragic relationships—his mother and father, who loved and tormented each other; his older brother, who loved and corrupted him and died of alcoholism in middle age; and O'Neill himself, caught and torn between love for and rage at all three.

O'Neill's final years were spent in grim frustration. Unable to work, he longed for his death and sat waiting for it in a Boston hotel, seeing no one except his doctor, a nurse, and his third wife. O'Neill died as broken and tragic a figure as any he had created for the stage. He was the first American dramatist to regard the stage as a literary medium and the only American playwright ever to receive the Nobel Prize for Literature. Through his efforts, the American theater grew up during the 1920s, developing into a cultural medium that could take its place with the best in American fiction, painting, and music.

ANNA AKHMATOVA

(b. June 11 [June 23, New Style], 1889, Bolshoy Fontan, near Odessa, Ukraine, Russian Empire—d. March 5, 1966, Domodedovo, near Moscow, Russia, U.S.S.R.)

The Russian poet Anna Akhmatova (the pseudonym of Anna Andreyevna Gorenko) was recognized at her death as the greatest woman poet in Russian literature.

Akhmatova began writing verse at age 11 and at 21 joined a group of St. Petersburg poets, the Acmeists. To their program of concrete representation and precise form and meaning Akhmatova added her own stamp of elegant colloquialism and the psychological sophistication of a young cosmopolitan woman, fully in control of the subtle verbal and gestural vocabulary of modern intimacies and romance. Her first collections, *Vecher* (1912; "Evening") and *Chyotki* (1914; "Rosary"), especially the latter, brought her fame and made her poetic voice emblematic of the experience of her generation.

During World War I and following the Revolution of 1917, she added to her main theme some civic, patriotic, and religious motifs but did not sacrifice her personal intensity or artistic conscience. Her artistry and increasing control of her medium were particularly prominent in her next collections: *Belaya staya* (1917; "The White Flock"), *Podorozhnik* (1921; "Plantain"), and *Anno Domini MCMXXI* (1921). The broadening of her thematic range, however, did not prevent the communist cultural watchdogs from proclaiming her "bourgeois and aristocratic" and condemning her poetry for its narrow preoccupation with love and God. In 1923 she entered a period of almost complete poetic silence and literary ostracism, and no volume of her poetry appeared in the Soviet Union until 1940. In September 1941, following the German invasion, Akhmatova was permitted to deliver an inspiring radio address to the women of Leningrad (St. Petersburg). Evacuated to Tashkent, Uzbekistan, soon thereafter, she read her poems to hospitalized soldiers and published a number of war-inspired poems; a small volume of selected poetry appeared in Tashkent in 1943. At the end of the war she returned to Leningrad, where her poems began to appear in local magazines and newspapers. She gave poetic readings, and plans were made for publication of a large edition of her works.

In August 1946, however, she was harshly denounced by the Central Committee of the Communist Party for her "eroticism, mysticism, and political indifference." She was expelled from the Union of Soviet Writers; an unreleased book of her poems, already in print, was destroyed; and none of her work appeared in print for three years.

Then, in 1950, a number of her poems eulogizing Stalin and Soviet communism were printed in several issues of the illustrated weekly magazine *Ogonyok* ("The Little Light") under the title *Iz tsikla "Slava miru"* ("From the Cycle 'Glory to Peace'"). This uncharacteristic capitulation to the Soviet dictator was motivated by Akhmatova's desire to propitiate Stalin and win the freedom of her son, who had been arrested in 1949 and exiled to Siberia. The tone of these poems (those glorifying Stalin were omitted from Soviet editions of Akhmatova's works published after his death) is far different from the moving and universalized lyrical cycle, *Rekviem* ("Requiem"), composed between 1935 and 1940 and occasioned by Akhmatova's grief over an earlier arrest and imprisonment of her son in 1938. This masterpiece—a poetic monument to the sufferings of the Soviet people during Stalin's terror—was published in Russia for the first time in 1989.

Akhmatova's longest work and perhaps her masterpiece, *Poema bez geroya* ("Poem Without a Hero"), on which she worked from 1940 to 1962, was not published in the Soviet Union until 1976. This difficult and complex work, in which the life of St. Petersburg bohemia in pre–World War I years is "double-exposed" onto the tragedies and suffering of the post-1917 decades, is a powerful lyric summation of Akhmatova's philosophy and her own definitive statement on the meaning of her life and poetic achievement.

In 1964 she was awarded the Etna-Taormina prize, an international poetry prize awarded in Italy, and in 1965 she received an honorary doctoral degree from the University of Oxford. Her journeys to Sicily and England to receive these honors were her first travel outside her homeland since 1912.

WILLIAM FAULKNER

(b. Sept. 25, 1897, New Albany, Miss., U.S.—d. July 6, 1962, Byhalia, Miss.)

William Faulkner was an American novelist and short-story writer who was awarded the 1949 Nobel Prize for Literature.

A reluctant student, Faulkner left high school in Oxford, Miss., without graduating but devoted himself to "undirected reading." In July 1918, impelled by dreams of martial glory and by despair at a broken love affair, Faulkner joined the British Royal Air Force (RAF) as a cadet pilot under training in Canada, although the November 1918 armistice intervened before he could finish ground school, let alone fly or reach Europe. After returning home, he enrolled for a few university courses, published poems and drawings in campus newspapers, and acted out a self-dramatizing role as a poet who had seen wartime service.

His first novel, *Soldiers' Pay* (1926), given a Southern though not a Mississippian setting, was an impressive achievement, stylistically ambitious and strongly evocative of the sense of alienation experienced by soldiers returning from World War I to a civilian world of which they seemed no longer a part. Back in Oxford—with occasional visits to Pascagoula on the Gulf Coast—Faulkner again worked at a series of temporary jobs but was chiefly concerned with proving himself as a professional writer. None of his short stories was accepted, however, and he was especially shaken by his difficulty in finding a publisher for *Flags in the Dust* (published posthumously, 1973), a long, leisurely novel, drawing extensively on local observation and his own family history, that he had confidently counted upon to establish his reputation and career. When the novel eventually did appear, severely truncated, as *Sartoris* in 1929, it created in print for the first time that densely imagined world of Jefferson and Yoknapatawpha County—based partly on Ripley but chiefly on Oxford and Lafayette county and characterized by frequent recurrences of the same characters, places, and themes—which Faulkner was to use as the setting for so many subsequent novels and stories.

In *The Sound and the Fury* (1929), his first major novel, he combined a Yoknapatawpha setting with radical technical experimentation. In successive "stream-of-consciousness" monologues the three brothers of Candace (Caddy) Compson—Benjy the idiot, Quentin the disturbed Harvard undergraduate, and Jason the embittered local businessman—expose their differing obsessions with their sister and their loveless relationships with their parents. A fourth section, narrated as if authorially, provides new perspectives on some of the central characters, including Dilsey, the Compsons' black servant, and moves toward a powerful yet essentially unresolved conclusion. Faulkner's next novel, the brilliant tragicomedy called *As I Lay Dying*

(1930), is centered upon the conflicts within the "poor white" Bundren family as it makes its slow and difficult way to Jefferson to bury its matriarch's malodorously decaying corpse. Entirely narrated by the various Bundrens and people encountered on their journey, it is the most systematically multi-voiced of Faulkner's novels and marks the culmination of his early post-Joycean experimentalism.

Absalom, Absalom! (1936) was Faulkner's next major novel. Because this profoundly Southern story is constructed—speculatively, conflictingly, and inconclusively—by a series of narrators with sharply divergent self-interested perspectives, *Absalom, Absalom!* is often seen, in its infinite open-endedness, as Faulkner's supreme "modernist" fiction, focused above all on the processes of its own telling.

Other novels followed in the late 1930s and early 1940s, but Faulkner's American reputation—which had always lagged well behind his reputation in Europe—was boosted by *The Portable Faulkner* (1946), an anthology skillfully edited by Malcolm Cowley in accordance with the arresting if questionable thesis that Faulkner was deliberately constructing a historically based "legend" of the South. Faulkner's *Collected Stories* (1950), impressive in both quantity and quality, was also well received, and later in 1950 the award of the Nobel Prize for Literature catapulted the author instantly to the peak of world fame and enabled him to affirm, in a famous acceptance speech, his belief in the survival of the human race, even in an atomic age, and in the importance of the artist to that survival.

The Nobel Prize had a major impact on Faulkner's private life. Confident now of his reputation and future sales, he became less consistently "driven" as a writer than in earlier years and allowed himself more personal freedom, drinking heavily at times and indulging in a number of extramarital affairs—his opportunities in these directions being considerably enhanced by several overseas trips (most notably to Japan in 1955) undertaken on behalf of the U.S. State Department. He took his "ambassadorial" duties seriously, speaking frequently in public and to interviewers, and also became politically active at home, taking positions on major racial issues in the vain hope of finding middle ground between entrenched Southern conservatives and interventionist Northern liberals.

The quality of Faulkner's writing is often said to have declined in the wake of the Nobel Prize, although *Requiem for a Nun* (1951) and *A Fable* (1954) suggest otherwise. He died of a heart attack in July 1962, at the age of 64, his health undermined by his drinking and by too many falls from horses too big for him.

VLADIMIR NABOKOV

(b. April 22, 1899, St. Petersburg, Russia—d. July 2, 1977, Montreux, Switz.)

Vladimir Vladimirovich Nabokov was a Russian-born American novelist and critic, the foremost of the post-1917 émigré authors. He wrote in both Russian and English, and his best works, including *Lolita* (1955), feature stylish, intricate literary effects.

Nabokov was born into an old aristocratic family. In 1922, after the family had settled in Berlin, Nabokov's father was assassinated by a reactionary rightist while shielding another man at a public meeting. Nabokov published two collections of verse, *Poems* (1916) and *Two Paths* (1918), before leaving Russia in 1919. He and his family eventually made their way to England, and he attended Trinity College, Cambridge, on a scholarship provided for the sons of prominent Russians in exile. While at

Cambridge he first studied zoology but soon switched to French and Russian literature; he graduated with first-class honors in 1922. While still in England he continued to write poetry, mainly in Russian but also in English, and two collections of his Russian poetry, *The Cluster* and *The Empyrean Path*, appeared in 1923.

Between 1922 and 1940, Nabokov lived in Germany and France. By 1925 he settled upon prose as his main genre. His first short story had already been published in Berlin in 1924. His first novel, the autobiographical *Mashenka* (*Mary*), appeared in 1926; his second novel, *King, Queen, Knave*, which appeared in 1928, marked his turn to a highly stylized form that characterized his art thereafter.

During his years of European emigration, Nabokov lived in a state of happy and continual semipenury. All of his Russian novels were published in very small editions in Berlin and Paris. His first two novels had German translations, and the money he obtained for them he used for butterfly-hunting expeditions (he eventually published 18 scientific papers on entomology). But until his best-seller *Lolita*, no book he wrote in Russian or English produced more than a few hundred dollars. During the period in which he wrote his first eight novels, he made his living in Berlin and later in Paris by giving lessons in tennis, Russian, and English and from occasional walk-on parts in films. Even after great wealth came to him with the success of *Lolita* and the subsequent interest in his previous work, Nabokov and his family (he and his wife had one son, Dmitri) chose to live (from 1959) in genteelly shabby quarters in a Swiss hotel.

The subject matter of Nabokov's novels is principally the problem of art itself presented in various figurative disguises. The same may be said of his plays, *Sobytiye* ("The Event"), published in 1938, and *The Waltz Invention*. The problem of art again appears in Nabokov's best novel in

Russian, *The Gift*, the story of a young artist's development in the spectral world of post–World War I Berlin. This novel, with its reliance on literary parody, was a turning point. Serious use of parody thereafter became a key device in Nabokov's art. His first novels in English, *The Real Life of Sebastian Knight* (1941) and *Bend Sinister* (1947), do not rank with his best Russian work. *Pale Fire* (1962), however, a novel consisting of a long poem and a commentary on it by a mad literary pedant, extends and completes Nabokov's mastery of unorthodox structure, first shown in *The Gift* and present also in *Solus Rex*, a Russian novel that began to appear serially in 1940 but was never completed. *Lolita* (1955), with its antihero, Humbert Humbert, who is possessed by an overpowering desire for very young girls, is yet another of Nabokov's subtle allegories: love examined in the light of its seeming opposite, lechery. *Ada* (1969), Nabokov's 17th and longest novel, is a parody of the family chronicle form. All of his earlier themes come into play in the novel, and, because the work is a medley of Russian, French, and English, it is his most difficult work.

Nabokov's major critical works are an irreverent book about Nikolay Gogol (1944) and a monumental four-volume translation of, and commentary on, Pushkin's *Eugene Onegin* (1964). What he called the "present, final version" of the autobiographical *Speak, Memory*, concerning his European years, was published in 1967, after which he began work on a sequel, *Speak On, Memory*, concerning the American years.

As Nabokov's reputation grew in the 1930s so did the ferocity of the attacks made upon him. His idiosyncratic, somewhat aloof style and unusual novelistic concerns were interpreted as snobbery by his detractors—although his best Russian critic, Vladislav Khodasevich, insisted that Nabokov's aristocratic view was appropriate to his subject matters: problems of art masked by allegory.

ERNEST HEMINGWAY

(b. July 21, 1899, Cicero [now in Oak Park], Ill., U.S.—d. July 2, 1961, Ketchum, Idaho)

Ernest Hemingway, an American novelist and short-story writer, was awarded the Nobel Prize for Literature in 1954. He was noted both for the intense masculinity of his writing and for his adventurous and widely publicized life. His succinct and lucid prose style exerted a powerful influence on American and British fiction in the 20th century.

Hemingway entered World War I as an ambulance driver for the American Red Cross. On July 8, 1918, not yet 19 years old, he was injured on the Austro-Italian front at Fossalta di Piave. He was decorated for heroism.

After recuperating at home, Hemingway sailed for France as a foreign correspondent for the *Toronto Star*. Advised and encouraged by other American writers in Paris—F. Scott Fitzgerald, Gertrude Stein, Ezra Pound—he began to see his nonjournalistic work appear in print there, and in 1925 his first important book, a collection of stories called *In Our Time*, was published in New York City; it was originally released in Paris in 1924. In 1926 he published *The Sun Also Rises*, a novel with which he scored his first solid success.

The writing of books occupied Hemingway for most of the postwar years. He remained based in Paris, but he traveled widely for the skiing, bullfighting, fishing, and hunting that by then had become part of his life and formed the background for much of his writing. His position as a master of short fiction had been advanced by *Men Without Women* in 1927 and thoroughly established with the stories in *Winner Take Nothing* in 1933. At least in the public view, however, the novel *A Farewell to Arms* (1929) overshadowed such works. Reaching back to his

The sparse yet pointed style of writing evidenced in Ernest Hemingway's novels may have been a holdover from the author's days as a journalist and war correspondent.

experience as a young soldier in Italy, Hemingway developed a grim but lyrical novel of great power, fusing love story with war story.

Hemingway's love of Spain and his passion for bullfighting resulted in *Death in the Afternoon* (1932), a learned study of a spectacle he saw more as tragic ceremony than as sport. A minor novel of 1937 called *To Have and Have Not* is about a Caribbean desperado and is set against a background of lower-class violence and upper-class decadence in Key West during the Great Depression.

By now Spain was in the midst of civil war. Still deeply attached to that country, Hemingway made four trips there, once more a correspondent. He also raised money for the Republicans in their struggle against the Nationalists under General Francisco Franco. The harvest of Hemingway's considerable experience of Spain in war and peace was the novel *For Whom the Bell Tolls* (1940), a substantial and impressive work that some critics consider his finest novel. It was also the most successful of all his books as measured in sales. Set during the Spanish Civil War, it tells of Robert Jordan, an American volunteer who is sent to join a guerrilla band behind the Nationalist lines in the Guadarrama Mountains. Through dialogue, flashbacks, and stories, Hemingway offers telling and vivid profiles of the Spanish character and unsparingly depicts the cruelty and inhumanity stirred up by the civil war.

Following World War II in Europe, which he experienced firsthand as a journalist, Hemingway returned to his home in Cuba and began to work seriously again. He also traveled widely, and, on a trip to Africa, he was injured in a plane crash. Soon after (in 1953), he received the Pulitzer Prize in fiction for *The Old Man and the Sea* (1952), a short heroic novel about an old Cuban fisherman who, after an extended struggle, hooks and boats a giant marlin only to have it eaten by voracious sharks during the long voyage home. This book, which played a role in gaining for Hemingway the Nobel Prize for Literature in 1954, was enthusiastically praised.

By 1960 Fidel Castro's revolution had driven Hemingway from Cuba. He settled in Ketchum, Idaho, and tried to lead his life and do his work as before. For a while he succeeded, but, anxiety-ridden and depressed, he was twice hospitalized at the Mayo Clinic in Rochester, Minnesota, where he received electroshock treatments. Two days after his return to the house in Ketchum, he took his life with a shotgun.

Hemingway's prose style was probably the most widely imitated of any in the 20th century. In striving to be as objective and honest as possible, Hemingway hit upon the device of describing a series of actions by using short, simple sentences from which all comment or emotional rhetoric has been eliminated. The resulting terse, concentrated prose is concrete and unemotional yet is often resonant and capable of conveying great irony through understatement.

GEORGE ORWELL

(b. 1903, Motīhāri, Bengal, India—d. Jan. 21, 1950, London, Eng.)

Eric Arthur Blair, better known by his pseudonym George Orwell, was an English novelist, essayist, and critic famous for his novels *Animal Farm* (1945) and *1984* (1949), the latter a profound anti-Utopian novel that examines the dangers of totalitarian rule.

Orwell was born in Bengal, into the class of sahibs. His father was a minor British official in the Indian civil service; his mother, of French extraction, was the daughter of an unsuccessful teak merchant in Burma. He won scholarships to two of England's leading schools, Winchester and

Eton, and chose the latter. He stayed from 1917 to 1921. Instead of accepting a scholarship to a university, Orwell decided to follow family tradition and, in 1922, went to Burma as assistant district superintendent in the Indian Imperial Police. When he realized how much against their will the Burmese were ruled by the British, he felt increasingly ashamed of his role as a colonial police officer. Later he was to recount his experiences and his reactions to imperial rule in his novel *Burmese Days* and in two brilliant autobiographical sketches, "Shooting an Elephant" and "A Hanging," classics of expository prose.

In 1927 Orwell, on leave to England, decided not to return to Burma, and on Jan. 1, 1928, he took the decisive step of resigning from the imperial police. Having felt guilty that the barriers of race and caste had prevented his mingling with the Burmese, he thought he could expiate some of his guilt by immersing himself in the life of the poor and outcast people of Europe. Donning ragged clothes, he went into the East End of London to live in cheap lodging houses among laborers and beggars. He spent a period in the slums of Paris and worked as a dishwasher in French hotels and restaurants, and tramped the roads of England with professional vagrants and joined the people of the London slums in their annual exodus to work in the Kentish hopfields.These experiences gave Orwell the material for *Down and Out in Paris and London* (1933), in which actual incidents are rearranged into something like fiction. The book's publication in 1933 earned him some initial literary recognition. Orwell's first novel, *Burmese Days* (1934), established the pattern of his subsequent fiction in its portrayal of a sensitive, conscientious, and emotionally isolated individual who is at odds with an oppressive or dishonest social environment.

Orwell's revulsion against imperialism led not only to

his personal rejection of the bourgeois lifestyle but to a political reorientation as well. Immediately after returning from Burma he called himself an anarchist and continued to do so for several years; during the 1930s, however, he began to consider himself a socialist. Orwell's first socialist book was an original and unorthodox political treatise entitled *The Road to Wigan Pier* (1937). It begins by describing his experiences when he went to live among the destitute and unemployed miners of northern England, sharing and observing their lives; it ends in a series of sharp criticisms of existing socialist movements. It combines mordant reporting with a tone of generous anger that was to characterize Orwell's subsequent writing.

In the 1940s Orwell was a prolific journalist, writing many newspaper articles and reviews, together with serious criticism, that combined patriotic sentiment with the advocacy of a libertarian, decentralist socialism. In 1944 Orwell finished *Animal Farm*, a political fable based on the story of the Russian Revolution and its betrayal by Joseph Stalin. In this book a group of barnyard animals overthrow and chase off their exploitative human masters and set up an egalitarian society of their own. When it appeared in 1945 *Animal Farm* made him famous and, for the first time, prosperous.

Orwell's last book, *1984* (1949), is a novel he wrote as a warning after years of brooding on the twin menaces of Nazism and Stalinism. The novel is set in an imaginary future in which the world is dominated by three perpetually warring totalitarian police states. Orwell's warning of the potential dangers of totalitarianism made a deep impression on his contemporaries and upon subsequent readers, and the book's title and many of its coined words and phrases ("Big Brother is watching you," "newspeak," "doublethink") became bywords for modern political abuses.

Orwell wrote the last pages of *1984* in a remote house on the Hebridean island of Jura, which he had bought from the proceeds of *Animal Farm*. He worked between bouts of hospitalization for tuberculosis, of which he died in a London hospital in January 1950.

Glossary

allegory: The use of fictional figures and actions to symbolize truths or generalizations about human existence.

archetypal: The original model on which representations of the same type are based.

dramatist: Someone who writes plays.

humanism: The belief that humans are basically good and problems can be solved by use of reason.

martial: Having to do with war or military life.

meter: The rhythmic arrangement of syllables in verse.

motif: A dominant or recurrent theme.

nihilism: A belief that existence is meaningless.

parody: Imitating a style in such a way as to mock it.

posthumous: Occurring after the death of a person.

prose: Writing that is not poetry.

sanatorium: An establishment that provides medical care and various treatments for the improvement of health.

satire: Something that makes fun of and shows the weaknesses of human nature.

treatise: A formal exposition in writing, generally longer and more specific than an essay.

For More Information

BOOKS

Eliot, T. S. *Old Possum's Book of Practical Cats*. London, UK: Faber and Faber, 2023.

Hemingway, Ernest. *The Old Man and the Sea*. London, UK: Vintage Books, 2022.

Woolf, Virginia. *Virginia Woolf: Quotes from a Feminist Icon*. London, UK: Laurence King Publishing, 2021.

Yeats, W. B. *The Poetry of W. B. Yeats*. London, UK: Sirius Publishing, 2023.

WEBSITES

Best Poems Encyclopedia

www.best-poems.net/anna_akhmatova/index.html

Learn about the life of Anna Akhmatova and read English translations of some of her most famous poems.

The Orwell Foundation

www.orwellfoundation.com/the-orwell-foundation/orwell/biography/

The Orwell Foundation provides a biography of George Orwell with descriptions of his literary achievements.

Poetry Foundation

www.poetryfoundation.org/poets/rabindranath-tagore

This site offers biographical information about Rabindranath Tagore and a selection of his poetry.

Poets.org

www.poetryfoundation.org/poets/robert-frost

Read a selection of poems by the famous American poet Robert Frost.

Index